THE
LAWS
OF
SPIRIT

Books by Dan Millman

The Peaceful Warrior Saga
Way of the Peaceful Warrior
Sacred Journey of the Peaceful Warrior

Guidebooks
No Ordinary Moments
Body Mind Mastery
The Life You Were Born to Live
The Laws of Spirit
Everyday Enlightenment
Divine Interventions
Living on Purpose

Especially for Children
Secret of the Peaceful Warrior
Quest for the Crystal Castle

For information about Dan Millman's work,
visit his website at
www.danmillman.com

THE
LAWS OF
SPIRIT

A Tale of Transformation

Dan Millman

H J KRAMER

NEW WORLD LIBRARY

An H J Kramer Book
published in a joint venture with
New World Library

Editorial office: Administrative office:
H J Kramer   New World Library
P.O. Box 1082   14 Pamaron Way
Tiburon, California 94920   Novato, California 94949

Editor: Nancy Grimley Carleton
Editorial Assistant: Claudette Charbonneau
Composition and Book Design: Classic Typography

Library of Congress Cataloging-in-publication Data
Millman, Dan.
    The laws of spirit : a tale of transformation / by Dan Millman.
      p.   cm.
    ISBN 0-915811-93-6
    1. Spiritual life. I. Title.
BL624.M4976   1995
291.4'4—dc20   95-19406
                                                       CIP

First hardcover printing, September 1995
First paperback printing, August 2001
ISBN 0-915811-93-6
Printed in Canada on acid-free paper
Distributed to the trade by Publishers Group West

10 9

There is a Mystery that many call God,
Manifesting as Universal Love,
a set of Laws,
and a Great Process.
That Process works through
each and all of us,
and that Process is perfect.
As we discover this fundamental truth
in the journey of our lives,
we find that wherever we step,
the path appears beneath our feet.

To Our Readers

The books we publish
are our contribution to
an emerging world based on
cooperation rather than on competition,
on affirmation of the human spirit rather
than on self-doubt, and on the certainty
that all humanity is connected.
Our goal is to touch as many
lives as possible with a
message of hope for
a better world.

Hal and Linda Kramer, Publishers

CONTENTS

ACKNOWLEDGMENTS

I use not only all the brains I have,
but all I can borrow.
—Woodrow Wilson

A book bears the author's name but represents a team effort; I borrowed from a wealth of talented professionals and friends, and wish to thank my editor and literary sculptor, Nancy Carleton; my friend and fellow writer, Doug Childers; my publishers, Hal and Linda Kramer; and the staff at H J Kramer Inc. My appreciation, also, to Dick Schuettge, Jim Marin, and Stan Shoptaugh, as well as Peter Russell, Holly Demé, Jerry Gregoire, David Kay, Jason Seeber, Wes Tabler, Fred Taub, Beth Wilson, and others who, in their own ways, helped give birth to this book. Finally, my deepest gratitude to my family for their support and understanding, and to a growing family of readers who inspire me to continue writing.

PREFACE

We cannot teach people anything;
we can only help them discover it
within themselves.
—Galileo Galilei

What are the most important principles for living you've learned? Some years ago, I asked myself this question. Since then, time and experience have provided answers and insights, leading to *The Laws of Spirit*.

The laws of Spirit belong to each of us. They are found within our hearts and lie at the heart of every religion, culture, and moral system. One method I use to access these universal laws is to ask, "If I met my Higher Self in the mountains, in the form of a wise being, what would that being teach me?" This question taps the wellspring of wisdom within us all.

All journeys are true, but not all are factual. In *The Laws of Spirit*, I present spiritual laws for life through a series of conversations and experiences with a fictional sage—a woman of extraordinary grace and understanding who teaches through vivid imagery from the natural world.

Unlike my previous full-length adventures, this book more closely resembles a parable than a novel. The archetypal figure of the mountain sage gives these simple yet powerful truths their own visceral and emotional reality. As the sage guides me along mountain paths, I invite my readers to travel with me and explore the most illuminating laws we are destined to master on the winding paths of life. These laws have expanded my perspectives and provided leverage to change the course of my life. I hope and trust they will do the same for you.

Dan Millman
Spring 1995

INTRODUCTION:
MEETING WITH A MOUNTAIN SAGE

We sit together,
the mountain and I,
until only the mountain remains.

—Li Po

Over the years, for health and enjoyment, I have often hiked into the wilderness near my home—up the narrow deer trails and down forested hillsides covered with oak, pine, and manzanita—wandering as impulse has taken me along the mountains leading to the coast.

On one such occasion, some years ago, when my family was away for a long weekend, I rose before dawn and set out without a plan except to climb at leisure and explore new country. The mountains, no more than a few thousand feet high, still had enough rises and dips to lose sight of civilization, evoking a sense of mystery and wonder as I imagined myself a hundred miles from anywhere.

The rolling hills reflected the peaks and valleys of my own inner life. At the moment, I felt lost in a valley filled with shadows of doubt. My life had fallen into an orderly routine. So on this particular morning I took with me into the hills an unspoken desire for excitement, for insight, for change. I was soon to discover the truth of the saying "Be careful what you ask for; you might get it."

On this morning, low clouds had drifted in from the coast to settle over the wilderness, and after I had hiked up some distance I found myself in a fold between the hills, enveloped in a fog so thick I could see no more than a few feet ahead. The air became cold and still, and I soon lost any sense of direction. Hearing a stream somewhere below, I kept it behind me, thinking I might climb up out of this shrouded valley.

I soon came to a plateau nestled beneath some ancient oaks just above a steep drop-off. I had, quite by accident, approached the plateau from the only possible angle—a narrow path between a wall of boulders. As I climbed around one of the massive stones, the fog disappeared to reveal a tiny hut standing before me. I approached and tapped lightly on the door.

To my surprise, a resonant voice rang out with unexpected warmth, as if I were a long-awaited guest: "Do come in, Traveler, come in!" And so, wandering off the beaten path of my life, I opened the door and found the sage, sitting quietly, smiling up at me. For no reason I could discern, goose bumps appeared on my arms.

She sat with a feline grace, erect yet relaxed, balanced upon a cushion of leaves on the earthen floor. She was dressed in a green tunic. Maybe she thinks she's in Sherwood Forest, I thought.

Her eyes held my attention – almond eyes, hazel colored, illumined by rays of sunlight shining through a crack in the wall – eyes set like jewels in a face of smooth olive skin, crowned by short brown hair that gave no clear sign of her age, race, or culture. She seemed to be surrounded by a bright field of energy, which I assumed was a trick of the light.

I began to feel oddly disoriented. I lost my bearings in time as well as space: Was this a primeval rain forest, a hillside in Shakespeare's England, the Scottish highlands, or a mountain abode of the Chinese immortals?

"A long time since I've had a visitor," she said. "I'm glad you have come, for I have much to share. And I need your assistance in a mission of great importance."

Was she lost? Did she need a guide? Puzzled but intrigued, I only said, "That sounds interesting."

"I believe you'll find it so," she replied. "But first you'll need some training – to prepare you."

"Prepare me? Uh, if this is going to take more than a couple of hours, I'm not sure I have the time."

"You have both less and more time than you imagine," she said – a strange response. Judging her odd but harmless, I decided to play along and see where this led. She gestured for me to sit down. "Make yourself comfortable, Traveler; I know why you have come and that you have journeyed far."

I was about to tell her that we were only an hour's hike from my home; then I sensed she was referring not to my morning's walk, but to the long and winding path of my life.

Abruptly, my mind was flooded with countless images, impressions of many different times and cultures. I had a strange sense that they were somehow connected with her. Then doubt entered my mind: Surely, I thought, she's just a reclusive woman and I'm weaving an adventure where there is none.

"Who are you?" I asked.

"A reflection in a quiet pond," she said. "A ray of moonlight on a dark night, as young as the morning dew and as old as the Earth. All things are in me, and I am in all things. Beyond that, Traveler, I cannot say, for my life is as mysterious as yours. The only difference between us is that I live in the embrace of a Spirit to which you are just awakening."

Speechless at first, I finally asked, "What should I call you? Do you have a name?"

"A name?" She looked genuinely surprised. "I've had so many names, I hardly remember."

"Well, what do you call yourself?"

"I hardly ever call myself," she replied with a smile. And that was that.

"Well, where do you come from?"

"I venture forth from the past and the future. I live in the eternal present. We've lost and found one another time and time again. I've worked with you in an old gas station and walked with you through the Hawaiian rain forest. I've lived in great cities. I've sat in high courts under arched domes lined with silver and gold. I've known the comforts of hearth and home and the solitude of the mountain monastery. I've labored in dusty fields, known the risk and riches of high enterprise, and felt the cold lash of poverty. I've walked beneath jeweled canopies of stars, through shadows cast by moonlight. I've traveled the seas, won and lost fortunes, known health and illness, pleasure and pain. And I have found treasures that would dazzle your eyes—luminescent silks, opals as large as fists, and sparkling gems of every color—but I would share with you the greatest treasure of all, a gift that grows in the giving and never loses its luster."

As she continued, her voice was the voice of All People, shifting like the wind, blowing through dusty hallways of history and places of radiant light. "Magic is alive in the world, Traveler. I intend to share with you the secrets of alchemy."

"Like turning lead into gold?"

She smiled. "Playing with minerals is a mere chemist's trick. The alchemy of which I speak can transmute the baser elements of your life – the fears, confusion, concerns, and difficulties you encounter – into the gold of freedom and clarity, serenity and joy. The laws of Spirit are the secrets I would share."

"You refer to 'Spirit' – do you believe in God? Do you have a religion?" I asked.

She smiled. "You don't have to believe in the sun to delight in the warmth of the morning light. It is simply obvious. That is how I know God. And as to my religion," she continued, gazing into the distance as if remembering times past, "I've sat in the shining temples of the Israelites and under the glorious spires of the mosques of Islam; I've knelt in the great cathedrals and bathed in the light of Christendom; I've sat in the sweat lodges and passed the pipe, lived as a shaman on the African plains, meditated in Buddhist temples, and inhaled the sweet aroma of incense on the banks of the Ganges. And everywhere, I've found the same Spirit in all religions – a Divine Will that transcends time, belief, and culture – revealing the universal laws that are the treasure of God."

"Can you say more about these laws?" I asked.

"I intend to," she answered. "Within the mystery of life, the universe operates according to laws as real as the law of gravity. Woven into the fabric of existence, reflecting the primal intelligence of the universe, these laws of Spirit direct the mechanics of the universe—the movements of flowers reaching toward the sun and waves thundering to the shore. They govern the movement of the Earth, the cycle of seasons, and the forces of nature. To their songs, even the galaxies dance."

With a puff of smoke and a strange whooshing sound, a small pile of branches and twigs in a circle of stones between us ignited, as if the flames had lit themselves. "Merlin taught me that," she said, her eyes twinkling. Even in my present state of awe, a skeptical part of me thought, Well, maybe it's Merlin, and maybe it's lighter fluid!

Then as we watched a thin plume of smoke drift up through the hut's thatched roof, she resumed speaking: "The laws of Spirit point to the innate order and intelligence of the universe. They transcend concepts, customs, and beliefs. They form the basis of all human morality. Constant as the movement of the planets, they apply not only to the mechanics of nature, but to every aspect of existence. They can guide you through the shallows and reefs of your life the way the stars and compass guided ancient mariners on their course.

"Certain laws," she added, "have special relevance to the practical affairs of human life. The books and teachings of religion touch upon these great truths—

simple, powerful principles for finding inner peace in a difficult world. Those who follow the laws prosper and find fulfillment; those who ignore or resist them meet consequences that instruct them on their journey of awakening, so they can one day find peace in the light of higher understanding."

"Where did you learn these laws?" I asked.

"They reside inside each of us as a vast storehouse of intuitive wisdom. And they are also revealed everywhere in the natural world." Then, standing swiftly and gracefully, she walked to the door and beckoned me to follow. "Come, Traveler; let the mountains be your classroom."

I resolved to remember whatever laws she might teach me — these "treasures" she referred to — in order to share them with my children, and perhaps with others who might be interested. But I hadn't begun to realize their full impact, power, and magic. Even so, I knew something unusual was afoot when I stepped through the doorway of the hut and found myself a stone's throw from a large, placid pond I had not seen before.

THE LAW OF BALANCE

FINDING THE MIDDLE WAY

If gravity is the glue
that holds the universe together,
balance is the key
that unlocks its secrets.
Balance applies
to our body, mind, and emotions,
to all levels of our being.
It reminds us that anything we do,
we can overdo or underdo,
and that if the pendulum
of our lives or habits
swings too far to one side,
it will inevitably swing to the other.

Be humble for you are made of earth.
Be noble for you are made of stars.

—Serbian proverb

"We're downwind, so he doesn't yet sense our presence," said the sage softly, directing my gaze to the edge of the pond, where a white bird balanced perfectly on one leg. "Can you balance like that egret?" she asked.

"What, you mean stand on one leg?"

"I mean feel what the egret feels *inside.* Can you remain as calm in the midst of your everyday life?"

"Yes . . . maybe . . . I don't know. I'm still trying to figure out how we *got* here."

She repeated her question: "You don't often feel such serenity, do you?"

"Well, no, I suppose not."

"An honest answer and a good starting point," said the sage as she sat down on the sunny knoll overlooking the pond. "Consider, for a moment, the importance of balance in the natural order of human life. We are creatures of moderation: We can't swim as well as fish, run as fast as cheetahs, or lift as much as gorillas, but we have all these abilities in moderation, in balance."

The sage pointed again toward the snowy egret, still poised at the water's edge. "Every human body yearns for and thrives in a state of inner balance, inner peace. Can you feel this inside you now?"

The instant she placed her palm on my chest, I felt a profound sense of peace pervade my body and quiet my mind. "You feel it," she whispered.

"Yes." I sighed with pleasure.

"This feeling of serenity provides a reference point; it will increase your awareness of, and decrease your tolerance for, the imbalances you normally experience."

"In what way?"

"Well, you can understand how it does little good to advise tense people to relax if they don't know what 'relaxed' feels like. But once they experience a state of deep relaxation, they have a reference point; they can more easily notice tension as it arises and can take steps to release it. And once you know what true balance feels like, you'll begin to notice what's out of balance in *any* area of your life; this serves as an automatic signal to you to return to that centered place within. You apply the Law of Balance by noticing your imbalances."

"As simple as that?"

She laughed. "Very simple, but not always easy, because whatever physical or emotional state you're accustomed to feeling — even if it's tension or extreme imbalance — will feel normal to you. What many people call 'neurosis' is actually an imbalance or exaggeration of a thought, impulse, or emotion we all feel at times. So shifting to a state of true balance may actually feel odd at first."

"Then how can I make the shift toward true balance?"

A fish broke the surface of the pond, sending ripples radiating along its mirrored surface as the sage responded: "Go to that quiet place, that still pond inside you. Look. Listen. Pay attention to any ripples in your body or your life caused by doing *too much* or *too little* in areas of eating, drinking, exercise, work, or communication."

As I considered this, another thought arose. "With everything going on in the world today, spending all this energy looking inside and finding balance and serenity seems kind of self-centered."

Smiling, the sage beckoned me to walk with her around the pond. "Many people confuse 'self-centered' with 'being selfish,'" she said. "But once you find your own balance, you also find the inner peace and inner power to make a real difference in the world."

She bent over and picked up a thin, straight branch, several feet long, and proceeded to balance it upon one finger. The branch stood perfectly upright at first; then it began to move slightly to and fro, tilting forward then backward. "Desires and attachments pull you forward," she said. "Fear, resistance, and avoidance pull you backward. Extremes of any kind, even taking rigid sides on an issue, can drive you out of that balanced place that values all sides of any issue. Do you understand?"

"I think so, but I'm not sure," I answered.

"Good! That means you're ready to learn."

As we proceeded along the trail, I noticed that the sage stepped so lightly over fallen branches I could barely hear her footfalls; her own state of balance was exquisite. "Like all the laws I intend to share with you," she continued, "the Law of Balance is not just a philosophy but a way of life, with very practical applications." Seeing my blank look, she picked up a stone, handed it to me, and pointed to a scrub pine about thirty feet away. "See that tree trunk over there? Let's see you hit it with the stone."

I took a breath, aimed, and threw. I missed by a few feet to the left. She handed me another stone. I threw again and got a little closer, but still to the left of center. She then handed me four more stones, looked into my eyes, and spoke slowly. "It's important that you hit the tree trunk with one of these stones." I didn't understand why it was so important, but I knew she meant it; I felt my heartbeat quicken.

"Apply the Law of Balance!" she reminded me.

"How?"

"I've already told you that when you're out of balance, it feels normal to you. Because of this, you keep leaning toward the familiar side. So the fastest way to find center is to overcorrect—to deliberately practice the *opposite* of what you're used to doing. For example, if you speak too rapidly or too quietly for people to understand you, then you need to deliberately talk in a way that feels 'too slow' or 'too loud.'"

"And since I just threw too far left," I said, "I need to aim too far right. Right?"

"Right," she said.

"The thing is, I only have four tries remaining; I don't want to miss that tree to the left *or* to the right. I want to *hit* it."

"I'm sure you do. But once you've worked both sides, it's far easier to find center, whether you're aiming at trees or doing anything else."

"I understand," I said.

"*Doing* is understanding," she replied, pointing to the tree.

Doubtful, but willing to try, I deliberately aimed to the right; to my surprise, I missed to the left again.

"You see," said the sage. "Accustomed to what you usually do—to what feels normal—you undercorrected. That's why changing any habit feels difficult, and why many people learn so slowly. This time be daring! Make sure the next two throws are to the *right* of the tree!"

I made very sure: The first stone went a yard to the right; so did the second. "My last try," I said nervously.

"The Law of Balance will help you," she said, "and so will I." She led me toward the tree until I was only five feet away. "No one said you had to make life so difficult," she added with a smile. "If you notice you're too far away, go too close!"

Laughing, I hit the tree dead center.

As we proceeded along the path around the pond, the sage spoke about another aspect of this law: *"Balance begins with the breath,"* she said. "Taking in and letting go are the primal rhythms of life. Breathing in, you find inspiration; breathing out, you find release. Inspiring and expiring — birth and death with every breath.

"Feel your breath right now," she said. "Notice how, when the rhythms of your breathing are out of balance, your emotions are too. So when you feel anger, accept it fully, and bring the breath to balance. When you feel sorrow, embrace it tenderly, and bring the breath to balance. When you feel fear, honor it, and breathe deeply to find your balance.

"As you exhale, you give; as you inhale, you receive. If you receive more than you give, you feel that imbalance as a need to reciprocate and complete the circle of relationship. If you give more than you receive, you feel depleted, and eventually have nothing left to give."

"I've read about saints who gave much and received very little."

"So it may appear, but such beings experience abundant joy, love, and gratitude," she responded. "The Law of Balance assures us that those who give freely, in the spirit of love and generosity, receive in abundance."

As we hiked onward up a winding deer trail into the hills, I remembered something she had said when we first met. "Earlier you said you needed my assistance," I said, "with some kind of mission."

"This is your preparation," she reminded me. "First learn the egret's lesson. Find balance in your life and in all things. Honor this law, and follow in the footsteps of the wise. Explore the range of human experience, but since habitual extremes create stress, always return to the golden mean, the middle way. Let your actions and words come forth softly, like the changing seasons. From that inner state of balance, you'll find clarity and peace."

As the sage's words faded into silence, and we continued up into the hills, I turned for a last glance at the egret, still standing in calm repose at the water's edge.

THE LAW OF CHOICES

RECLAIMING OUR POWER

We are both burdened and blessed by
the great responsibility of free will—
the power of choice.
Our future is determined, in large part,
by the choices we make now.
We cannot always control our circumstances,
but we can and do choose
our response to whatever arises.
Reclaiming the power of choice,
we find the courage
to live fully in the world.

Afoot and light-hearted
I take to the open road,
Healthy, free, the world before me,
The long brown path
leading wherever I choose.

—Walt Whitman

The pond's mirrored surface, shining like polished glass, receded then disappeared as we hiked up over a small rise. Soon after, the trail widened and split into three paths. "You lead for a while," said the sage.

"But I don't know where we're going."

She looked at me and smiled. "An interesting belief, Traveler, but I think you've always known where you were going, whether or not you were aware of it. So, which path will you choose?"

"Does it make any difference?"

"Ultimately? Not at all," she replied. "In the end, all paths lead to the same destination. But one of *these* paths may lead into a green valley, another to a rocky peak, and the third into a dark woods. You can't be sure where each trail leads; still, you must make a choice."

I smiled at her. "I get the feeling you're making some kind of a point."

"Choose your path; then we'll talk."

"Okay. Let's go this way," I said, pointing.

"Well?" she said as if she hadn't heard me. "Are you going to choose?"

"I already did. I picked the center path."

Again she spoke as if deaf to my voice. "Our time together is limited, Traveler. I suggest you make your choice so we can be on our way."

"But I . . . " Suddenly, I understood, and I began walking up the center path.

"Just so! The Law of Choices tells us that decisions are not made with words, but with actions." Pointing skyward, the sage then asked, "Do you see the turkey vulture gliding above us?" As I nodded, she knelt down and pointed to a nearby spider in its web. "Like the soaring bird and the tiny spider, most of Earth's creatures have a narrow range of choices; they act through instinct and the call of their natures. But you have free will—the power of choice. Your life represents an exercise of this power, and your destiny is determined, in large part, by the choices you make now.

"Free will," she continued, "means that you can choose to abide by the laws that speak within your deepest intuition, or you can let impulses, fears, and habits run the show. If you sometimes resist or ignore higher wisdom in favor of immediate gratification, the consequences of your choices eventually guide you back toward alignment with the laws of Spirit; one choice leads to a sunlit path and another to hurdles and tests that instruct and strengthen you, so all things serve in their own ways."

"It doesn't always feel as if I've always chosen my directions in life; sometimes it feels more like fate."

"Most decisions are directed by subconscious wisdom. Your 'inner knower' has more information than your conscious mind can access, so there are times when, without knowing why, you attract people or experiences into your life that you don't consciously want, but that serve your highest good and learning."

"What about the poor, the abused, the hungry? Are you suggesting they somehow choose to suffer?"

The sage stopped and gazed into the darkening woods ahead. "Pain has many faces; even the wealthy know suffering. All anyone can do is to make the best possible choices available within a particular set of circumstances — choices toward life, toward love, toward service, toward connection. But no matter what life dishes out, *you* get to choose how you will *respond* internally: You can resist and resent it, bemoaning your fate, or you can face and embrace it, expanding into the moment."

"What about those who choose discomfort or hardship because they care about someone else?"

"If you willingly choose to set aside your personal desires for the welfare of children, loved ones, or others, that can represent a spiritual act of self-sacrifice. But if you feel like a martyr, it's time to take another look. Assuming too much responsibility for others deprives them of the lessons that arise from the choices they have made. Those in pain need our compassion and support, but if we carry the weight for them, we rob them of their strength and self-respect."

I considered her words as we hiked up the path in silence. Then another question struck me: "There are times I wonder about the choices I've made—about my relationships, my work—"

The sage interrupted. "When you return home, I suggest you ask your wife for a divorce."

"*What?* What are you talking about?"

"Why not get a divorce? You have the power to do so at any time. You just call an attorney—"

It was my turn to interrupt. "I couldn't do that!"

"Why?"

"Because it would cause a lot of pain. For my wife. For my children. And for me. The finances would be a mess. And besides, I made a promise when we got married. I made a commitment. And what kind of example would that be to my kids?"

"So you're trapped," she said.

"I'm not trapped!"

"You certainly sound as if you are," she said lightly. "You gave a number of reasons—very good ones, I'm sure—why you *can't* get a divorce. But only when you reclaim the power to end your relationship can you fully commit to it. Only then can you passionately *choose* to remain married instead of 'having to' for one reason or another. Do you understand?"

"Yes," I said, smiling. "I think I do."

"And I'm not just talking about your relationships," she said. "This is about your work, your friends, your location, and your life."

"I don't understand."

"Just as some people, having forgotten their power of choice, feel trapped in a relationship, others feel trapped by their life or by circumstances, and things have to get very painful before they find the will, the courage, and the self-respect to make new choices.

"Unless you realize you have the power to say no," she continued, "you can never really say yes. To your relationships. To your work. To your life. To anything. You don't *have* to wait to make positive, empowering changes. You don't *have* to go to school; you don't *have* to go to work; you don't *have* to go to war; you don't *have* to be married, or have children, or act as other people expect or desire.

You don't *have* to do anything. Just recognize that every action or inaction has consequences, and that your willingness to accept these consequences gives you the power and freedom to choose who you are, where you are, and what you will do. That's when life changes from an obligation to a blessed opportunity. That's when miracles happen."

The path I had chosen took us deep into the woods, beneath a thick canopy of fragrant trees. In that sheltered place, as the wind whispered through the branches overhead, the sage shared her final words on the Law of Choices: "Realizing your power to choose and to change your directions in any moment, without regard to external pressures or ideals, is like rising up toward the surface of the sea after a long submersion. This power may intoxicate you as you see attractive alternatives to your present situation. You may feel tempted to change your relationship, your career, or any area of life that feels difficult or frustrating. Some new choices may be appropriate or even overdue, but the heroic choice often means taking responsibility for where you are now and participating fully and intentionally, with greater presence and passion than ever before.

"And the more you honor the Law of Choices," the sage continued, "the more you'll live with clear intention— *creating* your life—and instead of wondering if you are on the right path, with the right person, or doing the right job, you'll live each day by choice, and to the fullest."

As I considered the choices of my life, and how they had brought me here, I thought also of my work and family, reminding me of the home I'd left nearly eight hours ago. I found myself saying, "I'm very grateful for what you've shown me, but I should return home soon. There are things I have to do around the house."

She shrugged. "Choice means giving up something you want for something else you want more. It's your life; take off whenever you choose."

I'd half expected her to try to convince me to stay longer, and her detachment caught me off guard. I had a strange feeling that if I left there would be no coming back. "I—I guess I can stay a while longer," I replied.

"You don't sound very sure."

"No, I am, really. I *want* to stay; I just hadn't expected to be gone this long, and I had some plans."

The sage just smiled as if she knew me better than I knew myself, which was entirely possible.

As the trees opened to an expanse of hillside, I was treated to a wide panorama that matched my expanding awareness. It struck me as odd that I saw none of the familiar houses or city beyond, but here, with this woman, this *being*, I felt as if I were in another realm, and for all I knew, the passage of time here was but the blink of an eye in my everyday world. "Let's continue our journey," said the sage, already turning up a steepening path.

THE LAW OF PROCESS

TAKING LIFE STEP-BY-STEP

*Process transforms any journey
into a series of small steps,
taken one by one,
to reach any goal.
Process transcends time,
teaches patience,
rests on a solid foundation
of careful preparation,
and embodies trust
in our unfolding potential.*

We rise to great heights
by a winding staircase.
—Francis Bacon

*T*he trail inclined so sharply that I felt as if we were walking up a steep stairwell, straight up the mountain. Although accustomed to hiking, on this grade I felt my heart beat faster and my breathing deepen. The sage, however, seemed unaffected, and spoke without effort. "Have you noticed how this mountain path mirrors the journeys of life—how each day we climb toward our goals?"

"I hadn't noticed a path," I replied, panting, as I looked up toward the summit. "But I did notice that the peak doesn't seem to be getting any closer."

"If one focuses only on the journey's end, completion always appears in the distance. This leads many to abandon their goals when obstacles arise or the path grows steep. You know that every journey begins with a single step, but you also have to take a second step, and a third, and as many as needed to reach your destination. The Law of Process," said the sage, "is nature's assurance that we can achieve nearly any goal, no matter how lofty, by breaking it down into small, sure steps."

"That seems kind of obvious."

"*Completely* obvious," she agreed. "That's why so many people overlook it."

"You said that by taking small steps we can reach *nearly* any goal?"

"Well," she said, smiling, "you can't cross a chasm in two leaps. But you *can* apply a step-by-step process to prepare. And since we don't have any chasms handy . . ." The sage picked up a stone, handed it to me, and pointed to an oak tree about twenty yards distant. "Do you think you can hit that trunk?"

"What! From sixty feet away? I sincerely doubt it. Even if I aim to the left, then to the right, it's just too far."

"Okay, then," she replied, leading me directly to the tree until it loomed in front of us. "How about now?"

"Of course I can hit it, now."

"Then do it."

So I did, whereupon she took me one foot farther away, handed me another rock, and said, "Again." In this manner, by stepping one foot back each time, I succeeded with every throw until we were about twelve yards away, when I missed. "Step one foot forward and throw again," she said. My stone hit dead center. We continued backward, until I missed twice at sixteen yards, stepped forward one foot, then hit it again. Finally, after a few misses, I actually hit the tree from twenty yards.

As we forged once again up the steep trail, she continued her instruction. "You see how this law works in any area of life? By breaking any task into manageable steps, you don't have to wait for success at journey's end; you create a series of many small successes along the way."

We came to a wide stream swelled by the spring rains. The sage crossed first, walking lightly across a zigzag path of stepping-stones. I followed, hopping from one stone to the next. Seeing two stones close together, I made a quick decision and leaped for the farther one, landed a little short, slipped on some moss, and ended up in the stream. Making no effort to suppress a grin, the sage reached out with a hand. "So you see in any process, even crossing a stream, if you skip steps, sooner or later you're going to get wet."

The path began to widen, so we could walk side by side. Before long, just as my clothes were about dry, we came to a muddy bog. I looked right and left for a way around, but the sides of the little canyon were steep on either side. The sage threw back her head and laughed. "Nature is such a wondrous classroom! Her lessons appear at just the right time."

"Meaning?"

"Open your eyes!" she said. "How does this muddy trail reflect your life?"

"Right now I haven't a clue!"

"Let me spell it out. On the path stretching between you and your goals, do you usually find a red carpet?"

"No. More often I find a swamp."

"Yes. Worthwhile goals demand effort, risk, and sacrifice. You have to persist through fear and doubt; you have to draw on inner resources and become more than you were before. Every new challenge serves as an initiation: You meet discouragement; you overcome discomfort, boredom, and frustration; and you find out what you're made of."

As we sloshed ankle-deep through the mud, she added, "What pulls you through the muddy paths of life is the vision that inspired you to begin the quest. It can draw you like a magnet through the muck and mire. So the first step in any process is creating a direction, choosing a goal that shines for you."

"That's sometimes a tough question for me—deciding what goal to pursue."

"Well, you won't discover it by waiting for divine revelation, absolute certainty, a mystical vision, or the voice of God. So don't weigh ideas or wonder; don't doubt your direction or depend on others to tell you what you should or shouldn't do. Go toward what attracts or excites or inspires you—toward what touches your heart. Ask yourself what's worth the effort and the sacrifices that come with commitment to any goal."

As we washed off our muddy feet and shoes in a stream, the sage offered some advice: "Remember, Traveler, that lofty dreams in the distant future are a difficult burden to carry. The best goals may be those you can handle in the next week, the next day, the next hour, or the next step; create a process that yields many small successes."

"Many small successes," I repeated to myself as we continued up a ravine. "But what about people who seem to achieve fame overnight? Where was their process?" I asked the sage.

"Any truly successful venture," she responded, "is like building a house; it begins with a strong foundation and proceeds patiently toward completion. Some houses or careers are built quickly, but without a stable foundation; they look beautiful, but they don't stand for long. If you look closely at 'overnight successes,' you'll find that they usually took about ten years of preparation."

"Ten years . . ." I said, mostly to myself.

"Think of it!" she said. "In ten years, you can accomplish nearly anything. You can become a physician or a scientist. You can develop high-level skills in a sport, game, or martial art. You can become an expert on any subject. You can create wealth or transform your body."

"Ten years still seems like a long time!"

"Looking forward, yes; but looking backward, centuries pass in the snap of a finger, in the blink of an eye."

Abruptly, she pointed skyward. "Look! Up there, at the summit." I looked; it still seemed far away. "Now look back," she said. I turned to view the hills below. "We've come a long way, step-by-step. We've been walking and talking for hours. That might have sounded like a long time if I had told you when we began. But looking back—"

I finished her sentence. "It doesn't seem long at all."

We headed up through the clump of trees into a darkly shaded area, losing sight of the sky. The sage knelt down and picked up an acorn and explained, "The same way this tiny acorn grows into a towering oak, the same way a river patiently carves a canyon from stone, the same way you've grown from a helpless infant into a mature man, you can and will accomplish all that you desire, one step at a time."

"You make it sound so certain. How can you be sure? After all, even going step-by-step, one can still fail."

"Few things are certain in this world," she said, "but people rarely ever fail; they only stop trying." As we stepped out from the cover of trees into a larger canopy of sky, we turned and looked at the hills below as the sage offered some final words on the Law of Process.

"Lasting progress doesn't happen in a few dramatic moments, but hour by hour, day by day. And as time passes, every process includes repairs: The road to happiness is always under construction. Focus on taking life one step at a time until you get it right; set aside what you can do later. When discipline and patience join forces, they become a persistence that endures past the peaks and valleys to carry intentions to completion. Enthusiasm sets the pace, but persistence reaches the goal. Process, patience, and persistence are keys that unlock the doorway to any destination. The treasure isn't only at journey's end, you see; the process itself is its own reward."

We found ourselves standing on the summit. Wiping my brow, I surveyed the magnificent view below, all the sweeter for having been earned. I looked toward the sage as she pointed toward yet another, higher peak in the distance, and another beyond. "Reach one goal, and you only create another; the journey never ends," she said as we turned back down the mountain.

THE LAW OF PRESENCE

LIVING IN THE MOMENT

Time is a paradox,
stretching between a "past" and "future"
that have no reality
except in our own minds.
The idea of time
is a convention of thought and language,
a social agreement.
Here is the deeper truth:
We have only this moment.

*It's only possible to live happily ever after
on a moment-to-moment basis.*

—Margaret Bonnano

Our hike down went more quickly than the climb up, but I was so lost in thought that I hardly noticed. Where are we going? What will we be doing next? Will I be able to remember what she is telling me? When will I get home? Will I see her tomorrow?

As if in response to my inner pondering, she said, "You seem preoccupied. So perhaps now is a good time to describe the Law of Presence. Yes," she reflected, "*now* is always a good time." The sage pointed out over the hills below, then asked, "Do you see how the sun illuminates that field of daffodils—there, against the emerald grasses? To me they're as beautiful as any work of art in any museum of the world." We walked in silence as the colors slipped from the twilight sky.

A few minutes later, as we rounded a wall of familiar boulders, her hut came into view. The sage opened her thatched door and once again invited me inside. She quickly set the fire to crackling. Then she stood and excused herself to go outside — I assumed to take care of her physical needs as I had done earlier.

As the minutes passed and she did not reappear, I began to fidget, wondering when she would be back and how I would find my way home in the dark — if, indeed, I returned home at all tonight. I supposed I could always sleep in the hills; the temperature was cool but not cold, and my family would not return until Monday afternoon, two days hence.

What happened next was so bizarre that I began to doubt my senses. Instead of the sage, a large cat entered the hut. She walked in deliberately, as if she knew exactly where she was going. She had a dark, shiny coat, part Siamese, maybe, and part — well, part sage. I say this because the next thing I knew, she spoke to me — not with her mouth, but with her mind. Her voice was like that of the sage, only quieter. She sat tall, as cats do, looked right at me, and got to the point. "Have you ever considered how time is a paradox?" she asked before daintily licking the fur on her shoulder.

Feeling very strange, I answered aloud, "I can't say that I have. Not since reading my last time-travel novel, anyway."

Her voice again resonated in my ears or my mind: "Time stretches between a past and a future that have no objective reality. Time is a convention of thought and language, a social agreement."

"In other words, time exists because we say it does?"

"Exactly so," she whispered. "Time is like a film of your life that consists of separate frames passing in front of a lens. Each frame is where you exist, in a present moment, but the frames appear to move. You can project your mind into what you call the past or the future, but you cannot live in any moment other than the present. I and my kind are masters of the present moment." Having said this, she stretched, lay down gracefully, and attended to her fur.

I considered what she had said. I'd always liked cats, despite their air of aloof superiority. And as crazy as it seemed to learn the Law of Presence from a cat, it also felt completely appropriate. No cat I have ever known gave much due to past or future. Like the wisest of sages, cats live each moment afresh.

The cat looked up at me with complete attention. "I, and my kind, have presence because I am totally present. Here and now. Can you say the same?"

"Me? Well, yes. I—I sometimes feel like I'm right here. That is . . ." By the time I had stammered this far, she had turned to more important things, like watching a moth in the light of the fire.

As if I hadn't said anything worth a comment, she

continued. "What you did this morning or yesterday or last year has now vanished, except in your mind. What is to come is only a dream. We have only this moment, you see."

"I see!" I said, not at all sure of what I saw.

"I'm not done. Are you aware that your sense of time passing is only an array of impressions and memories happening in the present moment? Regrets of the past are present impressions happening now. Future anxieties have no reality except in your mind, in this moment, as images, sounds, and feelings. In other words, past and future are happening *now* as you create them."

In a vague attempt to get some high ground, I said, "If this is the Law of Presence, it seems rather abstract."

"*Time* is the abstraction," she replied. "However, you can apply the Law of Presence in very practical ways to banish regrets, concerns, or confusion. Your ability to refocus attention back to the present moment grows with practice. Someday, you may be able to do this as I do, quite naturally."

So much for high ground, I thought. This cat had a point. And she clearly practiced what she preached. Then my mind drifted for a moment, and I looked toward the door. Where was the sage? She should have been back long ago.

"*Hellooo!*" I heard the cat say, snapping me back to the

present. "Do you understand how the Law of Presence can change your life forever? 'Forever,' of course, being right now."

"I already know the value of living in the present," I retorted, trying to salvage a little self-respect.

"Knowing and doing aren't necessarily the same thing, especially in your case," she purred, looking extremely pleased with herself. "Whenever you have a problem, it involves something past or future. You keep problems alive in your present mind by giving them your attention and energy, letting them live rent free in your head. I, in contrast, don't give them the time of day. Life's too short," she said with finality.

"Well, thank you, Your Highness," I said. "Are you finished?"

"Not by a long shot. Not until you truly understand that past and future are nothing more than a bad habit of the mind – of *your* mind. Concerns about past or future are like the delusions of a crazy man who hears voices or sees creatures that exist only in his imagination, present company excluded, of course."

The irony of hearing this from a talking cat did not escape me.

"But," she continued, "as you notice what you're doing more and more, you can overcome this habit as you might any other, by remembering and applying the Law of

Presence." She stopped licking her fur and gave me her undivided attention. "I sincerely hope you appreciate the Law of Presence and the time I've taken to explain it to you." Without waiting for my response, she continued: "Presence is like a time machine that lightens the mind, liberates you from anxiety, and gives birth to a new way of living. In other words, you become more like me."

"I can hardly wait," I said, then laughed.

"As I've said, in order to *have* presence, you have to *be* present and remember where you are and *when* you are; then you will know *who* you are. Presence teaches that what you do today is important, because you are trading a day of your life for it. So let this law sweep your mind clear of unnecessary debris and return you to a state of clarity, simplicity, and inner peace."

"Like you," I volunteered.

"I'm so glad you noticed," she purred. "And remember that no matter how real or compelling your thoughts may be, you can always call upon the Law of Presence, reminding yourself that only now exists, that only now is real. If you do so as an act of reverence, making the moment sacred, you bow to that quiet, catlike self inside that knows, and all is well."

"So it's that easy to become catlike?"

"It may be a considerable stretch, in your case," she said, arching her back, yawning, and walking around the fire toward the door. "Embrace this moment, put one foot in front of the other, and handle what's in front of you. Because no matter where your mind may roam, your body always remains here and now. When in haste, rest in the present. Take a deep breath, and come back to here and now." The cat once again stretched luxuriously, and, without another word, walked out the door.

Almost as soon as the cat left, the sage reappeared and sat down, without explanation. "Where was I?" she said. "Ah, yes, we were discussing the Law of Presence."

"I think that was covered pretty well," I said. Did I detect something like amusement in her eyes? "And where have you been?" I asked.

"Oh, outside, enjoying the night air — leaning against the back of the hut there, behind you."

"But — wait a minute, were you . . . ?" I didn't even bother to finish. I just watched as the sage, with great presence, put a small kettle suspended on a green stick over the fire, and dropped in some tea leaves. I wondered whether we would be talking into the night, but then I let it go and enjoyed the moment — and the tea, which, as it turned out, was superb.

THE LAW OF COMPASSION

AWAKENING OUR HUMANITY

The universe does not judge us;
it only provides consequences and lessons
and opportunities to balance and learn
through the law of cause and effect.
Compassion is the recognition that
we are each doing the best we can
within the limits
of our current beliefs and capacities.

That I feed the hungry,
forgive an insult, and love my enemy—
these are great virtues.
But what if I should discover
that the poorest of the beggars
and most impudent of offenders
are all within me,
and that I stand in need
of the alms of my own kindness;
that I myself am the enemy
who must be loved-
what then?

−C. G. Jung

Gazing over the small fire, I could see the flames reflected in the sage's eyes. Her face, now illuminated by the firelight, appeared ageless, except for a few lines around the eyes — from smiling, I supposed. She smiled often, so that even when she seemed deeply serious, I could detect an underlying sense of humor and perspective.

After we spent some time in silence, gazing into the burning embers, she invited me outside to learn the Law of Compassion. We rose together and stepped through the doorway.

I looked around in wonder. Had the terrain changed again, or was it a trick of the moonlight? Before us lay a level area with enough trees to offer shelter from a misting rain that settled the day's dust and carried a pleasant, earthy odor of bark and leaves mixed with soil and grasses.

"Everything feels so alive," I remarked.

"And so it is," she responded as she caressed the rough bark of a nearby tree. In the light of a waxing moon, the rolling hills became curves on the Earth's body. "Extend your mind far beyond these hills," she continued. "Reach across the oceans, the fjords, the volcanoes, the reefs, the towering mountains above and beneath the sea, all teeming with life, all of it – the flesh and bones, the blood and spirit of the Earth, our mother."

She held up her finger to show me a tiny flea, which leaped up and disappeared. "If you were a flea," she said, "standing on the back of an elephant, you would see only a forest of great hairs growing around you, with no idea what you actually stood upon. But if you leaped high into the air and looked back, you'd see that you actually lived on the skin of a living creature. This is what happened to the astronauts who first soared into space: They left Earth as scientists and pilots and came back as mystics, because they saw the vision of a single, glorious, sacred, blue-green, living, breathing planet. This vision brings humility, and with it, a sense of awe and compassion that carries into the affairs of ordinary life.

"Just as you can learn balance from an egret and presence from a cat, you can learn the Law of Compassion from the Earth on whose skin we tread, whose trees we cut and burn, whose living wealth we exploit, going about our business without ever thinking of asking permission or giving thanks."

The sage looked up into the night sky. "For many centuries, I've spoken with the Earth. I know her heart, and I say to you that she understands in a way so deep and profound that tears would come to your eyes if you could but touch the edges of her compassion. The Earth forgives us because she knows that we are flesh of her flesh — we are a part of her that is still learning and growing.

"And so I ask you this," she continued, squatting down, taking some rich soil in her hands, and letting it run through her fingers, "if the Earth can forgive you for your mistakes, can you not forgive yourself, and offer others the same compassion?"

I lay back and looked up at the starry sky. "I don't think I'm all that good at compassion."

"You don't give much of it to yourself, do you?" she asked gently.

"No, I don't suppose I do."

"Then that's where to begin; the more loving-kindness you give to yourself, the more you can give to others." She rose and walked back inside the hut. I followed. Gazing at me over the crackling fire, with a light in her eyes, the sage revealed the heart of this law. "The time has come, Traveler, for you to see yourself and others in a new way, free of the judgments and expectations that come between you and the world. The time has come to understand that all of us — friends and adversaries alike — are doing the best we know how within the limits of our beliefs and capacities.

"The poet Rumi once wrote, 'Out beyond ideas of wrongdoing and rightdoing, there is a field. I'll meet you there. When the soul lies down in that grass, the world is too full to talk about.' Rumi could write these words because he understood that judgments are a human invention — that God is not here to judge us, but to provide us the means to learn from our errors so that we can grow and evolve." The sage turned to me and asked, "If you can accept that God doesn't judge you, why should you judge others?"

"I try not to judge others," I said, "but what about violent or cruel people?"

"The Law of Compassion is not arbitrary or conditional," she said. "We know that deeply troubled and destructive people do exist in this world, and that disturbed people tend to disturb others. Compassion doesn't mean letting such people walk over you or continue their destructive behaviors; some individuals need to be separated from society. But one can have compassion for evil without succumbing to it. In battle, you can feel compassionate toward your adversaries even when fighting to the death."

"But why feel compassion for cruel or despicable people? Why not just hate what is hateful?"

"That is an important question, and deserves a clear answer—an answer you must find for yourself. But consider this: Hate and compassion are different kinds of energy; which do you want to fill your world?"

"I can't argue with your goodwill," I responded, "but I still find it very difficult to feel kindly toward bigots or those who prey on children."

"I never said that compassion was easy!" she said. "But easy or not, the law directs you to act out of love and understanding rather than out of hatred or ignorance. To do so requires a leap to a larger perspective—to the realization that you live in a universe as just as it is mysterious. This depth of understanding flows from intuitive insight into the inherent intelligence of the universe. Whether you find such understanding through observation, reason, or religious faith, it reveals, finally, that in the natural world you have no friends, you have no enemies. You only have teachers."

"It seems like one has to be a saint to practice this law."

Smiling, she answered, "The Law of Compassion presents a loving demand to transcend our limited perspectives. This can feel overwhelming at times. So remember that compassion starts with yourself. Be gentle and patient. We each have many thoughts and feelings, both positive and negative, that arise in the mind and heart. You don't have to be a saint, but instead of believing or resisting the negative thoughts, let compassion wash them away in a wave of love and understanding."

"It still sounds pretty saintly."

The sage stood and paced for a few moments before turning to face me. "Can you remember a time in your life when you were in the midst of a heated argument—when you felt resentful, envious, or betrayed?"

"Yes," I said.

"Go back to one of those times," she said, "and feel the pain and anger."

"Okay. I feel it."

"Now imagine, in the midst of this heated argument, that the person you're arguing with suddenly clutches his or her heart, utters a cry, and falls dead at your feet."

"My God," I said, picturing what she had asked.

"Where is your anger now? Where is your envy and jealousy, your resentment and pain?"

"Those feelings are gone," I answered. "But—but what

if I were glad they were dead? What if I couldn't forgive them?"

"Then you can forgive yourself for not forgiving them. And in that forgiveness you'll find the compassion that heals the pain of being a human in this world. To call forth such forgiveness when you need it," she added, "remember to imagine your friend, lover, or adversary lying dead at your feet as you will one day lie at the feet of Spirit. Then you will see through different eyes, because death is the great equalizer. We are all going to depart this world and leave those we love. We all feel hope and despair; we all share dreams and loss. We are all joined without knowing why, in the mystery of life, doing the best we can."

"Maybe that's what Plato was saying when he wrote, 'Be kind, for everyone you meet is fighting a hard battle.'"

"Yes," said the sage. "Now you understand." With that, she walked over to a bed of leaves and lay down. I watched her for a few moments, in the fading glow of the fire, as the last embers flickered and died.

THE LAW OF FAITH

TRUSTING IN SPIRIT

Faith is our direct link to universal wisdom,
reminding us that we know more
than we have heard or read or studied—
that we have only to look, listen,
and trust the love and wisdom
of the Universal Spirit
working through us all.

Faith dares the soul
to go farther than it can see.
–William Clarke

When I awoke she was gone, and I had no idea whether she would return. I rose quickly, stepped outside, and looked for her, but I could find no sign, not even a footprint. As the minutes passed, doubts drifted like dark clouds across my mind. Did she really exist, or was it all some kind of wondrous dream? No, of course it had been real, and good, and true.

Then, as I scanned the woods, I caught sight of her, standing in the quiet morning shadows next to three deer—a doe and two fawns. In that moment, she seemed one of them, a deer in human form, and I felt like an outsider. They turned at the same time and saw me. The deer stepped into the deeper cover of the trees and disappeared as the sage approached me.

"There's something I'd like to show you," she said, giving me a handful of the season's early blackberries. "The deer like them, but you may find them bitter." She was right; still, they satisfied my hunger and filled me with a sense of lightness and vitality. Then we were off on a morning hike. Stopping only to drink with cupped hands from a small waterfall, I followed her, stride for stride, onto a small grassy knoll, where there grew a colorful field of flowers—reds, yellows, and dazzling blues.

"Watching blossoms open to the morning light reminds me of the Law of Faith," said the sage.

"Is this law about religion?" I asked.

"Faith doesn't require a belief in an external God—only a belief in flowers," she said, smiling. "But if one appreciates flowers, one must certainly appreciate God—not as a belief, but as a feeling of wonder and mystery. The Law of Faith is about trusting the inherent love and intelligence working through you and all creation."

"Well, I can't honestly say I trust everyone."

The sage laughed. "Faith is not blind. We all know of people who are dishonest or dangerous, and so we need to be strong and vigilant in this world. That's why an Arab sage once offered the reminder 'Trust in Allah, but tie your camel.'

"Practicing the Law of Faith doesn't mean trusting every person to do the right thing. It has a higher, more transcendent meaning: Faith is the recognition that Spirit works in, as, and through each and all of us—through every person and every circumstance. Faith is also an attitude that whatever happens serves a higher good, despite appearances to the contrary."

"That's kind of a stretch, isn't it? Especially if one experiences a tragedy."

"Faith is one of the greatest stretches, one of the greatest leaps, a human being can take. Because all you have to go on is, well, faith."

"So how do I make that leap?"

The sage sat down, settling like a leaf on the grassy slope, and asked me, "What if you suddenly knew with *certainty* that a higher intelligence was working through you and everyone else for the highest good of humanity—that there is indeed a purpose for every pleasure and hardship?"

"If I *knew* that, it would make a difference."

"The Law of Faith doesn't require you to believe this, Traveler, but it guides you to live your life *as if* this were true; in other words, on faith. And as you live in the light of this law, it will transform your perception and experience of the world. You'll begin to see every difficulty as a test in order to instruct you; you'll find lessons and opportunities in every challenge."

"Are you suggesting that I value faith over reason?"

She laughed, apparently finding my comment amusing. "Faith is not the opposite of reason. Applying the Law of Faith is one of the most practical, reasonable, constructive things you can do to live an inspired life."

Reaching out to touch one of the flower petals, she added, "As one of nature's most delicate and vulnerable life forms, a flower's life is short and tenuous. A careless footfall, a dry winter, or pounding rain can make a life-and-death difference to a delicate blossom. And yet, each morning it opens wide. Flowers have much to teach us about faith. When you cultivate the garden of faith in your own life, you will, like this flower, come alive in a new way."

I looked down and touched the delicate blossom, so soft and so vulnerable. For the first time, I realized that I didn't have even the faith of a flower. The sage's next words responded precisely to my innermost feelings. "Faith is not a commodity that you own or possess," she said. "It's the divine order that pervades all things, the light behind your eyes, the loving and mysterious intelligence that emanates from the center of creation."

"How can I experience that kind of faith in my every-day life?" I asked.

"To begin, listen to the intuitive wisdom of your heart, where Spirit speaks. So many people rely on books, teachers, scientists, psychics, oracles, or others to advise or direct them, or to validate their views."

"But aren't I relying on your advice and direction?"

A light drizzle began to fall, turning to a downpour. The sage led me under the cover of overhanging branches as she responded. "Teachers and books have their value, and sources of guidance and inspiration may enter your life in different forms. But never forget that the treasure is already inside you; others cannot give you anything you don't already have; they can only provide keys to your own inner wealth. So listen well to those who speak from experience and embrace wisdom where you find it, but always weigh external guidance against the wisdom of your own heart."

"There are times I've trusted myself, made a decision, and been wrong."

"You may choose one path over another, then meet with great hardship and difficulty as a result of that decision. Does that necessarily mean it was the wrong choice in terms of your highest good and learning?"

"Well, no, I guess not."

"Faith is assuming that you always make the right choice."

"I'd love to have that much faith in myself."

"Self-trust," she offered, "develops naturally, from your own direct experience; you learn to trust your body's instincts, your heart's intuition, and your mind's ability to access universal intelligence."

As a light sprinkle of rain cooled my forehead, the sage pointed to water pouring out of a crack in a nearby rock, forming a waterfall that splashed onto the boulders below. "Do you see how the water appears to pour out of the rocks?" she asked. "Yet, you know that the water comes not from the rocks but through them—that the water's source is above. Like water, higher wisdom doesn't come as much *from* your brain as *through* it. You aren't a vessel to be filled with facts; you're more like a radio receiver attuned to the universal intelligence operating throughout creation. All you have to do is to listen and trust."

"I wish I were as certain of that as you," I said.

The sage smiled again. "Faith means living with uncertainty, Traveler—feeling your way through life, letting your heart guide you like a lantern in the dark. There is no absolute security except in absolute faith. This doesn't mean that all circumstances will go your way or that divine justice is operating every time you injure or heal yourself. All sorts of events, both beautiful and terrible, can happen in this world. Our small mind cannot always see the bigger picture or know what is for our highest good. So despite the confusion and insecurity of life, when you can learn to live on faith, like the flower, trusting Spirit working according to a higher will beyond the reach of your mind, you'll see Spirit operating everywhere, in everyone and everything.

For several minutes, as we hiked over a rise and down a curving trail, my mind rested in silence, until finally, another question arose. "When I'm able to access such inner wisdom, will I be guided, like you, and avoid making so many mistakes?"

She laughed. "A few weeks ago I tripped and fell halfway down the hill."

"Really?"

"Really. But while I was lying there, I found a beautiful stone I would have missed had I not fallen. So, you see, faith is not about being infallible and always having everything go your way. Faith involves the willingness to stretch yourself, make mistakes, and learn from them—in other words, to trust the process of your life. The more you trust Spirit in this way, the more you will work with it directly as a living force in your life."

As the sage finished speaking, the rain stopped. Stepping out from under some trees into the warm sunlight, I felt an extraordinary sense of calm and well-being. In that moment, I knew that despite the challenges and tests confronting humanity, our world was in the hands of Spirit, unfolding, like a flower, toward the Light.

THE LAW OF EXPECTATION

EXPANDING OUR REALITY

Energy follows thought;
we move toward, but not beyond,
what we can imagine.
What we assume, expect, or believe
creates and colors our experience.
By expanding our deepest beliefs
about what is possible,
we change our experience of life.

Our lives are shaped
not as much by our experience,
as by our expectations.
—George Bernard Shaw

We continued in silence along the winding deer trails until we reached a plateau, where the sage stopped abruptly. She handed me another stone and pointed toward a tree trunk about twenty feet away. "I have a challenge for you," she announced.

"Another tree?" I asked.

"Yes. But this time you have only one stone—one chance to hit the tree square on."

"And if I don't?"

"I have more treasures to share, but if you miss the tree, our time together is over," she said.

"You really mean that?"

"I mean everything I say."

"Why is it so important that I hit the tree in one try?" I asked, pointing toward it.

"Not that tree," she corrected me. "The other one,

over there." She pointed to a large oak, *ninety* feet away.

"I can't possibly hit that in one try! What about the Law of Process? Shouldn't I start closer?"

"This is not about the Law of Process. This is about the Law of Expectation — about how your underlying beliefs and assumptions shape your experience."

"Well, I admit it, then. I don't believe I can hit that tree."

"*I* believe you will," she said, smiling.

"If you believe it, then *you* hit it!" I replied, hefting the rock nervously.

Ignoring my comment, the sage sat down and invited me to do the same, but I declined. "I'd rather stand if you don't mind. I'm a little tense."

"Stay present," she reminded me. "You'll always have time to worry later on if you want to."

So I sat, and listened. "Before anything manifests in this world," she began, "it first appears as a thought or image in someone's mind. Your thoughts color the windows through which you see the world; your beliefs become the building blocks of experience. In other words, every positive thought is a prayer, and every prayer is answered."

"Do you really believe that?" I asked.

"What I believe is less important right now than what

you believe," she replied. "Not what you *think* you believe; such surface beliefs have little impact. Only your deepest underlying assumptions have the power to shape your reality."

"That reminds me of an old poem," I said. "'Two men looked through prison bars; one saw mud, the other saw stars.'"

"Yes," she said. "What you see depends upon where you choose to look, and where you look depends upon what you expect to see: If you believe, for example, that 'people can't be trusted,' you'll see the world through the filter of this expectation and find evidence that supports it. Your beliefs influence the choices you make, the directions you take, even the friends, adversaries, and destiny you meet. Your beliefs set into motion inner processes and behaviors that influence how you move, act, and feel. On more subtle levels, your thoughts even affect the size and color of your energy field, to which other people respond. If, for example, you perceive the people around you as friends who like you, you feel relaxed and expansive; your energy and behavior draw them to you. This is one way your expectations shape your reality."

"That all makes sense, and I can't *wait* to learn how this is going to help me hit that tree on my first try."

"Your *only* try," she corrected, gesturing for me to stand. "Now, focus all your attention on the tree, get ready to throw the stone, and say aloud, 'I can hit the tree with ease.'"

Feeling silly, I said, "Okay. I can hit the tree with ease." I didn't believe it for a second, of course. In fact, I was overcome by doubts: There was no way I could hit that tree at ninety feet the first try or probably any try—not if I threw left then right, not if I started up close, which she wouldn't let me do anyway, not if I were a major league pitcher. No one could be expected to do this; it was just too far!

"Hitting the tree is easy," said the sage, responding once again to my thoughts. "The challenge is overcoming the negative beliefs that hold you back."

She picked up a stone. My mouth dropped open as she flung the stone into space, hitting the tree dead center with a resounding whack. "That was just to get your attention," she said, smiling, while I stared, wide-eyed. "It isn't enough for you to repeat over and over, 'I can do it, I can do it,'" she explained, "not while your underlying doubts are stealing your spirit, robbing you of your focus and strength. I want you to bring these negative expectations into the open—into the light of conscious awareness where they can be seen for what they are. Go ahead, shout them out at the top of your lungs!"

I felt really stupid, but I did as she asked; I yelled out all the reasons I couldn't hit the tree. I voiced all my doubts, at her urging, again and again, out loud.

"Now," she said, "look at the tree again, and create this expectation: '*I can hit the tree with ease.*'"

So I said it again—"I can hit the tree with ease"—and the strangest thing happened: Not a single doubt came up. It was simply true. I *felt* it; I believed it, completely! It rang true and real. As I looked at the tree, I felt a line of energy stretching from me to the tree, and I knew the stone would follow that line to its target. I stood squarely, on balance. Nothing else existed but me and that stone and that tree. For an instant, there was no "me" left. That's when I took a breath and threw the stone. The moment I let it go, I *knew* it would hit its target. I saw it fly, attracted to the tree like a magnet. The stone hit the trunk dead center, and as it hit, something shifted inside me. I understood the Law of Expectation: Before I could do it, I had to believe it; I had to really expect it.

Nodding, the sage said, "Before you did it, you saw it happen in your mind. And in your daily life, if you create positive images, happy circumstances, and successful outcomes, these become real to your deeper mind, which builds upon such experiences to attract similar ones. The Law of Expectation reminds you of your inherent power to shape your·life through the images and expectations you create. By airing all your doubts, you root them up from the deeper mind so that they can dissolve in the light of awareness."

"What if I created the expectation that I could fly? Could I use the same process?"

"I don't want to dampen your enthusiasm, Traveler, but the laws of Spirit that manifest in this plane of reality are senior to our human beliefs; you see, gravity works whether you believe in it or not."

"So even if I banished all doubts, I still couldn't fly."

"But you *can* fly!" she said. "You can soar into the air, fly into space, and land on the moon! Enormous doubts and 'scientific fact' had to be overcome before humanity could do the 'impossible' and take flight. Within the laws of Spirit, there are no limits except our beliefs. Our future as individuals and as a species will mirror our ability to understand and apply the Law of Expectation."

As we hiked down into the valley, the sage continued. "The Law of Expectation highlights the importance of examining your old beliefs and assumptions, replacing self-defeating doubts with vivid images, and creating new beliefs based on clear intention."

"What if there's no evidence to support that belief?" I asked.

"That is what I have tried to express to you," she said. "Believe it anyway! The expectation will attract the evidence."

"I'll do my best," I replied. "But speaking of self-defeating doubts," I said, "reading the newspapers sometimes depresses me; it's easy to lose hope for humanity, with all our environmental problems, unwanted children, crime, and greed."

"I'm not filled with hope," said the sage. "I'm filled with faith. Real problems exist. But even as we address the issues that cry out for help, it seems wisest to focus on positive outcomes and on our human potential. The Law of Expectation teaches that what we focus on expands; fighting problems only strengthens them by giving them energy. So focus on the solutions, not on the problems."

The sage glanced up at a hawk above our upturned heads, floating like a kite on the wind, and shared a final reminder about the Law of Expectation. "Like the ancient alchemists, Traveler, you can transmute doubt into confidence, and fear into courage. New expectations breed new choices. Don't wait for experiences to confirm them. Create a new vision of who you would become, and you surely will become it."

THE LAW OF INTEGRITY

LIVING OUR TRUTH

*Integrity means living and acting
in alignment with spiritual law
and with our highest vision,
despite impulses to the contrary.
From the heart of integrity,
we recognize, accept, and express
our authentic interior reality,
inspiring others not with words,
but by our example.*

I am not bound to win
but I am bound to be true.
I am not bound to succeed
but I am bound to live up to
what light I have.

–Abraham Lincoln

After watching the hawk spiral upward on rising currents of air, we headed into a deep valley where the trees wore a lace of emerald moss. As we descended, I thought about the laws I had learned so far, but could recall few details.

Addressing my concern, the sage said, "You don't have to remember all the words, Traveler. Words are only sounds. Yet, some voices carry the power to penetrate the heart and touch the soul. You acquire this spiritual authority only by living the laws of Spirit."

Stopping, she gazed into the distance and pointed to a peak behind us. "Can you see the summit of that hill?"

"You don't want me to hit it with a rock, do you?"

She smiled. "No, nothing like that. I just want you to climb to the top and return here within thirty minutes."

I gazed up at the hilltop. "Thirty minutes? But even if I ran all the way there and back, I still doubt — I mean, I suppose I could work with my beliefs — "

"You have twenty-nine minutes left," she said.

I shut up and took off.

The run was difficult and painful. Halfway up, my lungs burned so badly that I considered turning back before I reached the top. I felt I couldn't go on, but I had to, so I did; I hit my wall and went through it.

When I returned, I nearly fell at her feet. I was ten minutes late. I was breathing hard and wondering what this failure meant, when the sage asked, "Why didn't you turn around before you reached the top? That way you could have gotten back on time. Who would have known the difference?"

"*I* would," I said, catching my breath. "*I* would have known."

She smiled broadly. "There you have it: The Law of Integrity is about living in line with your highest vision despite impulses to the contrary — about how you behave when no one is watching."

The sage led me, still soaking with perspiration, over a rise where we came to a seasonal pond, still full from winter rains. Without a trace of self-consciousness, she removed her outer clothing and entered the pond. I did the same. It was not my everyday experience to be alone in the mountains, nearly skinny-dipping with a woman other than my wife. The sage was attractive enough; I found myself wondering if she had a love life. I felt a twinge of guilt. Not that I had any sexual intentions—I did have my rules—but I can't say the thought didn't cross my mind.

Just then she turned toward me and spoke to my thoughts: "Breaking society's codes is like swimming upstream, against the current of contemporary values. It can be done if your heart's deepest desire will not be denied, but it makes life more difficult—even exhausting—and it has consequences."

"Such as?"

"Such as ruffling the beliefs and emotions of others who take those beliefs very seriously," she said.

"So integrity means following social conventions?"

"Following the conventions of your society and avoiding what is considered unethical, illegal, or immoral is not about integrity; it's about intelligence."

"So you recommend conformity because it's easier?"

"I'm not recommending that you blindly conform or blindly rebel. Just keep your eyes open, and pay more attention to your heart's highest wisdom than to indulging or denying random impulses or desires. Follow Martin

Luther's guidance on integrity: 'Love God and do as you please.' "

Do as you please, I thought, wondering for a moment whether this were some kind of invitation, and what I would do if it were. My ruminations were soon interrupted by the sage's words as she slipped back into her clothes and indicated that I should do the same. "As I was saying, Traveler, the Law of Integrity calls forth a genuine expression of our internal reality. It also recognizes that if envy, greed, and manipulation influence our actions or expression, the consequences are *inevitable*, built into the mechanics of the universe. In breaking spiritual law, *the act itself is the punishment*, setting into motion subtle forces whose consequences we cannot escape any more than we can escape the law of gravity."

By this time we had walked deeper into the valley, where steep hillsides and thick foliage muffled the sounds of our passing. Lost in thought about convention, desires, and integrity, I nearly collided with the sage, who had stopped to point at a lizard peeking out of a rock crevice. "That lizard is not trying to be something else," she said. Then she began pointing toward one object after the next, saying, "That is a tree. There is a brook—"

"Yes," I interrupted. "I see them."

"But can you *feel* them?"

"I'm not sure what you mean."

"Unlike the creatures of the natural world, humans are surrounded by social artifice, cut off from their own true natures."

Then, speaking almost in a whisper, she said, "The shamans—the healers of the native peoples—practice the art of shape-shifting. This art is not as much about changing your body as expanding your awareness into an animal, a tree, or a stream in order to feel them—to learn their lessons—identifying with each one so that you feel its inner qualities and 'become' it. This is possible because your larger Self contains all these things."

"What does this have to do with the Law of Integrity?"

"I thought you might ask," she said, smiling. "My friend Lao-tzu once said, 'The snow goose need not bathe to make itself white; nor must you do anything but be yourself.' The natural world is ripe with such authenticity; the rushing stream, the moving wind, and the chirping crickets are content to be themselves. Are you content to be who you are completely—to be nothing more, nothing less?"

"What if I want to become something more?" I asked.

"More?" The sage smiled. "How could you be more? You are already limitless, boundless! When you die, Traveler, no one at the gates of heaven will ask if you were a saint; they will ask you if you were *yourself.*

"The wisdom of the ages," she continued, "from Plato

to Shakespeare, reminds us, 'Know thyself,' and 'To thine own self be true.' Integrity means *being integrated*, knowing ourselves and being ourselves, so that our actions are authentic, consistent with our highest intentions – so that our body, mind, emotions, and attitudes complement one another, forming a whole that is greater than the sum of the parts.

"It's meaningless to speak of integrity until we understand our innermost drives, values, and motives – until we accept who we are rather than who we hope or pretend to be. One person may give to the poor out of love and compassion; another may give out of guilt, or the need to impress others. Each shows charity; only one shows integrity. Motives and intent make a vast difference in the lives of both givers and recipients, because we give far more than coins; we give the currency of the self."

"I'm getting the impression that integrity is a lot more difficult to achieve than I thought."

"Everything is difficult until it becomes easy," the sage replied. "It takes courage and openness to achieve authenticity – to be able to say to yourself and to the world, 'Like it or not, this is who I am,' and then to *live* that truth. But once you accept your humanity, integrity is not difficult at all. It's not about being perfect or infallible; we've all made mistakes. We can only do our best and learn from our mistakes, so we can do better next time. Alignment with the

Law of Integrity means acknowledging our weaknesses and drawing on our inner strengths, so we become examples who light the way for others."

"Maybe that's what Mahatma Gandhi meant when he said, 'My life is my teaching.'"

"Yes," she responded. "Children have never been very good at listening to their parents, but they never fail to imitate them."

"I don't think you're just talking about children."

"Indeed not," the sage replied. "We all influence one another by our example, and we all learn by imitation, whether or not we are conscious of it. We touch others not so much by what we say, but by how we live.

"I once walked down an isolated stretch of road with a woman who called herself Peace Pilgrim," the sage continued. "She traveled on faith, walking until offered shelter and fasting until given food, reminding us, 'Live according to your highest light and more light will be given.' This summarizes the essence of integrity, Traveler, and this you are called upon to practice."

THE LAW OF ACTION

MOVING INTO LIFE

No matter what we feel or know,
no matter what our potential gifts or talents,
only action brings them to life.
Many of us understand concepts
such as commitment, courage, and love,
but we truly know only when we can do.
Doing leads to understanding,
and action turns knowledge to wisdom.

You can't cross the sea
merely by staring at the water.

—Rabindranath Tagore

Emerging from the valley, we climbed a short, steep incline and ended up on a rise just above the sage's hut. My stomach growled. Except for a handful of berries, I hadn't eaten in nearly two days. Just then the sage announced, "It's time we ate."

"Funny," I said. "I was just thinking about that—"

"I know," she said. "I could hear your stomach rumbling." Smiling, she led me to a garden she had cultivated. A brook flowed through it, which she had used to irrigate the colorful herbs, fruits, and vegetables growing there. "Pick whatever appeals to you."

We cooked squash and potato, spiced with bittersweet parsley and some other herbs I didn't recognize, served with a fresh salad. As we sat down to eat, the sage spoke of the Law of Action. "You can't eat good intentions," she began. "To prepare this meal, I cleared the land, dug the soil, and sowed the seeds before reaping the harvest. It takes more than dreams and good intentions to live in this world; it takes action."

As we ate, she told me of an incident—from a former life, I supposed. "I didn't always appreciate the difference between ideas and action," said the sage. "As a young scholar in India, I learned a valuable lesson. At that time, I came from a privileged family, spending most of my time reading. One day, while on a journey, as the boatman took me across a wide river, I described to him how I had gathered all my knowledge. The boatman listened attentively; then, after a time, he asked me if I could swim. 'No,' I replied, 'I cannot.' 'Then I'm afraid your knowledge is wasted,' said the boatman. 'This boat is sinking.'"

We both laughed as her point struck home.

"Well, what happened?" I asked her.

"Oh, I drowned," she answered. "It was a lesson I would never forget. This world is a realm of energy and action; no matter what you know or who you are—no matter how many books you have read or what your talents only action brings potential to life. Philosophies impress and ideas abound, but words, no matter how elegant, are cheap. It's easy to speak about commitment, courage, and love, but *doing* is understanding, and wisdom grows out of practice."

I followed her as she walked to the far edge of the

garden, climbed some boulders, and surveyed the expanse of forest below.

"Many people would enjoy such a view," said the sage. "They might aspire to make the climb and might desire the satisfaction of standing here. But they didn't reach the top or enjoy the view, and we are—not because we are smarter or stronger or more deserving, but because we made the climb. Only those who make the climb get to enjoy the summit."

Later, as we returned to our meal, the sage observed, "Taking action has never been easy in this world; forces of doubt and inertia are everywhere, even within our mind and body. Turning ideas into action requires energy, sacrifice, courage, and heart, because to act is to risk. We have to overcome all the good reasons to put it off, to let someone else do it, to remain in the easy chair of good intentions. But the Law of Action delivers the same message again and again: It's better to do what is best than not do it and have a good excuse."

"It seems to me that just getting out of bed in the morning takes courage, so everyone applies the Law of Action."

"All living beings act, but most people react—and then only when compelled by pain or fear, when relationships break into warfare or when bodies become ill from stress. The Law of Action teaches us to overcome both inertia and impatience by acting out of courage, clear intention, and commitment."

"So how does one overcome inertia?"

"By acknowledging three fundamental realities," she replied. "First, by accepting our humanity and our physical presence in the world; second, by realizing that no one is going to live for us and that we only grow stronger from our own efforts; and third, by accepting that action may entail discomfort—and then getting on with it!

"We no longer have the luxury of waiting until we feel safe and secure, inspired or motivated—until fear or doubt is looking the other way. We can no longer wait for someone to give us permission to act. I feel a great urgency. That's why I've appeared again, in this time and place—why I'm speaking to you now. The time has come to act in line with our highest ideals, despite fears, doubts, or uncertainties that arise. We can only show courage in the face of fear. Every day we need courage, because every day we face fears—not necessarily in dramatic ways like tackling a bank robber or saving a drowning person, but in expressing our feelings, breaking an old habit, or taking the risk to be different."

We stood and began to clean up what little remained of our meal. "I like to scatter the scraps as an offering to the animals, but not too near the hut." She led me through some trees to the edge of a hillside so steep it almost qualified as a cliff.

Standing at the edge of the precipice, the sage began throwing a few scraps down for the deer grazing far below. Suddenly, the hillside on which she stood, soft from heavy rains, gave way. Before my shocked eyes, she disappeared from sight. I lunged forward and saw her tumbling down. I found myself leaping over the edge, trying to maintain my balance as I slid after her. We were now both sliding toward a vertical drop-off.

She must have been conscious, because I saw her grabbing at tree roots, trying to slow herself down. It all happened as if in slow motion, in crisp detail. I knew I was getting bruised and scraped, but I felt no pain.

I wanted to help her if I could, but first I had to help myself; I began grabbing at roots and grasses. Luck was with me, and, as I fell past her, we clasped hands. That must have been when the falling stone glanced off my head, because I remembered nothing more.

I woke up lying next to a pond. My head was wet with blood. I opened my eyes and saw the sage, her face dirty but smiling as she wiped my head with a wet cloth. "The bleeding's stopped," she said. "It looks like you're going to live."

"You, too," I said, managing to return her smile.

Later, in the chill of evening as we huddled by the fire back in her hut, I reflected upon what had happened, and fear finally hit me: "We could have been killed! Or *I* could have been killed—I don't know about you."

"You would have been a little wiser and a lot safer if you had stayed where you were," she responded. "But you showed courage in coming after me."

"I wasn't being courageous; I didn't think about it. I just saw you fall, and I jumped."

"Still, a perfect demonstration of the Law of Action."

"If you need any future demonstrations, I'd prefer throwing rocks at trees."

She smiled. "Sometimes these things happen."

"Well, it must be your year for falling down hills," I said, referring to the earlier fall she had told me about.

"Do you think it's a sign for me to live closer to sea level?" she asked. Then, more serious, she added, "It could have gone the other way. You might have gotten yourself killed. Your impulse to help was both commendable and shortsighted."

"*What?*"

"You assumed that I couldn't help myself."

"Well, you did look like you needed a little help."

"And so I did. Still, be aware that every law contains the seeds of its opposite. Sometimes compassion demands action, but this law also teaches the wisdom of remaining still and quiet, the action of nonaction."

"Like meditation," I said.

"Yes. There is a time for action and a time for stillness. You can sometimes show the greatest courage, patience, and wisdom by remaining still even when compelling desires or impulses urge you to act."

"How can one know when to act and when to be still?"

"Those who tend toward inertia or fear need to focus on the will to act bravely and decisively. Those given to impulsive speech or action are wise to stop, take a few breaths, and observe their impulses without feeling compelled to act on them. In any case, listen to the wisdom of your heart; then you'll know when to remain still and when to seize the moment."

After that, we sat together in the stillness of the evening, staring into the flames as the fire's warmth drew out the soreness of our recent adventure. As the evening grew dark, weariness pulled me toward sleep. I lay on my side, gazing into the flames and listening to her voice: "Fire transforms matter into energy, reminding us that all things pass and change. In the end, we are each consumed by the flameless fires of life. So act bravely, Traveler, while you still have the time, while you still have a body." After that came silence.

THE LAW OF CYCLES

DANCING TO NATURE'S SONG

The world of nature moves
in rhythms, patterns, and cycles—
the passing of the seasons,
the movement of the stars,
the ebb and flow of the tides.
The seasons do not push one another;
neither do clouds race the wind across the sky.
All things happen in
their own good time—
rising and falling and rising
like ocean waves,
in the circles of time.

In every winter's heart
lies a quivering spring,
and behind the veil of each night
waits a smiling dawn.
—Kahlil Gibran

That night in the hut, I had a vivid dream; at least I think it was a dream: I was awakened by the sage's voice. It was already light outside, even though it seemed I had just fallen asleep. I felt no soreness from my earlier fall; in fact, I hardly felt my body at all. The sage said, "Come." I don't remember her lips moving. Then I was standing by the door of the hut, staring out at a bright summer day. The California grass had turned brown, and the air was dry and dusty.

"Close your eyes," she said. I remember a few moments of total darkness and silence. Then my eyes opened to a cloudy autumn day. An early rain must have fallen, for the dust had settled and the dry grass showed traces of green. A cool wind gusted in my face, so I shut my eyes.

When I opened them, I felt the crisp chill of winter;

the trees that weren't evergreen were bare. Traces of frost lay across fallen leaves. I stepped outside, felt the hard, cold earth, and heard thunder in the distance.

In a flash of light, the air changed to spring once again, and I heard the sage's voice. "The natural world dances to the music of change—the passing of the seasons, the revolutions of the heavens, and day turning to night. All things happen in their own good time, changing and growing, appearing and disappearing, waxing and waning, the ebb and flow. Whatever rises will fall, and whatever falls shall rise again. This is the Law of Cycles."

Then it was morning. I awoke refreshed but decidedly sore. After I splashed cold water on my face and ate a few berries, the sage invited me to walk with her to a special place higher in the hills. As we hiked up a rocky trail, I told her about the dream.

"The seasons have much to teach you, and your dream is a sign that you're ready to understand."

"Understand what?"

"That the winds of change may come as a fierce hurricane, ripping your life asunder, or as a tender breeze that caresses your cheeks—that change is the only constant, and that it happens in its own way, in its own time."

"I've always had mixed feelings about change. Sometimes, when life feels dull, I wish for it, but when things are going well, difficult change can feel—well, difficult."

"Change itself isn't difficult," replied the sage. "It happens as naturally as a sunrise. But most of us seek familiar routines to create a sense of control and order, so change can feel like a blessing or a curse, depending on our desires; the same rain welcomed by the flowers is mourned by picnickers wishing for a sunny day.

"The Law of Cycles reminds us that as the seasons change, so must we, that our old habits don't have to run our lives, that our past doesn't have to become our future, and that the momentum of change ultimately leads us toward greater awareness, wisdom, and peace."

Looking back toward her lush garden, the sage added, "Gardening through the four seasons reveals other lessons of the natural world: that seeds only reproduce their own kind, that you reap only what you sow, that when you gather the harvest you need to save some seed for the next planting, that you have to end one cycle in order to begin another, that there is a time for all seeds to grow, change, and eventually die, to be plowed under for a fresh planting. As with seeds and cycles, so go our lives.

"Enjoy each season of your life, Traveler. Patiently prepare the soil, sow the seeds, and do the work, and you'll harvest the abundant fruits of your labors. Accept both good fortune and adversity as you accept the shifting seasons. Enjoy the glazed beauty of a winter's day and the sultry days of summer, for soon enough, each season, each

day, each moment, passes into history, and its exact like-
ness shall not be seen again. So rather than longing for
summer in the midst of winter's chill or wishing for cool
winds in the dog days of summer, embrace each season for
its own gifts. Align yourself with the cycles of time and
transformation, riding change as ships ride the waves."

"You're saying that cycles of change are going to happen whether I like it or not, so I might as well accept
them."

"That, and more," she replied. "The Law of Cycles
also reveals how to cooperate fully in your own evolution,
master good timing, and find good fortune."

"How so?"

"All things have a most favorable and a least favorable
time," she answered. "Doors open and close; energies rise
and fall. A thought or action initiated while energy is rising and gaining momentum travels along easily toward
completion, but a thought or action initiated in a descend-
ing cycle has a reduced impact. That's when the Law of
Cycles blends with the Law of Action to reveal that patience is the better part of wisdom—wisdom to know
when to act and when to keep still, when to talk and when
to be silent, when to work and when to rest, when to
ride the energy of a building cycle or go within and wait
for the next rising wave."

As we stepped off the trail and headed directly into

a thick growth of trees and brush, the sage paused for a moment and told me a story. "In the ancient days, King Solomon felt great inner turmoil and craved the return of simpler, more peaceful times, so he decreed that a master jeweler should make him a magical ring inscribed with words that would be true and appropriate at *all* times and under *all* conditions—words that would help to alleviate suffering and provide the bearer with great wisdom and perspective. This master jeweler crafted a special ring, but only after many days of contemplation did he divine the words of power. Finally, the jeweler presented the ring to Solomon. On it were inscribed the words 'And this too shall pass.'"

The terrain changed abruptly as we stepped out of the trees and came to a sunny clearing. I saw an orange tree, heavy with bright oranges that I could smell from where I stood, and several apple trees, blossoming but not yet ready to bear fruit, and two other trees I didn't recognize.

"They're walnut trees," said the sage, responding to my inner question, her timing perfect, as usual. Then, bowing respectfully to one of the walnut trees, she pulled a small green fruit from one of the branches and handed it to me. "Open it," she said.

"I don't think it's ready to eat yet."

"Open it," she repeated. I tried—first with my fingers, then by hitting the green husk between two stones. Finally,

I found a sharp stone and tried to chop it open, but with no success. When the sage tapped me on the shoulder, I turned to see that she had a handful of ripe walnut shells. "From last year's harvest," she said. "I had them stored nearby."

She took a small stone and gave the shell a light tap, and it popped right open. She did the same with more walnuts, and we enjoyed a filling snack. As we nibbled, she explained, "I am here to share with you simple truths for making life work better. But I cannot promise you enlightenment; that has its own timing. We humans, you see, are like the walnut shell: If you try to force it open at the wrong time, it's nearly impossible, but once it's ripe, you just tap at the right place, and it opens easily. Daily life is your ripening process. And one day, someone or something will come along and provide the tap."

We sat beneath the shade of the apple trees, eating walnuts and oranges as the sun rose toward the treetops. I leaned back against the apple tree and listened to the sounds of the nearby brook, feeling a kinship with the natural world. The sunshine warmed my bones, soothing me into a restful state of deep calm. I lay back, looked up through the shimmering leaves, and watched the clouds drift overhead. As if on cue, the sage said, "Notice how the clouds move easily with the wind, without haste or resistance?" This was an idea I had considered before, but her gentle voice, articulating my innermost thoughts, touched something deep inside me so that the clouds and the wind penetrated to the center of my awareness. In that moment, nature had become my teacher.

The sage finished her instruction about the Law of Cycles with a story: "Many years ago, while traveling in Poland, I visited the humble abode of a renowned rabbi known for his great wisdom. The single room in which he lived was filled with books. Other than that, he had nothing except a single table and a bench.

"'Rabbi,' I asked, 'where is your furniture?'

"'Where is yours?' he then asked me.

"'Mine?' I responded, puzzled. 'But I'm just passing through.'

"'So am I,' said the rabbi. 'So am I.'"

THE LAW OF SURRENDER

EMBRACING A HIGHER WILL

*Surrender means
accepting this moment,
this body, and this life
with open arms.
Surrender involves
getting out of our own way
and living in accord with
a higher will,
expressed as the wisdom of the heart.
Far more than passive acceptance,
surrender uses every challenge
as a means of spiritual growth
and expanded awareness.*

*Some think it's holding on
that makes one strong;
sometimes it's letting go.*
—Sylvia Robinson

*M*orning turned to afternoon. A sudden gust of wind rippled the branches over our heads, shaking loose a single leaf that twirled down to land in a nearby brook. Gesturing toward the rushing water, the sage asked, "Have you noticed, Traveler, how flowing water is soft yet powerful? Yielding, forceful, flexible, it surrenders to gravity without resistance, adapting to the shape of any container. Water reveals the most intelligent and powerful response you can make in any circumstance."

"And what response is that?"

"*Surrender,*" she said.

"I don't understand," I said. "I was taught to fight for what I believe in—to never give up."

"Although the Law of Surrender means accepting whatever happens in your life, it does *not* mean passive toleration for what you don't like, or ignoring injustice, or allowing yourself to be victimized or controlled. True surrender is active, positive, assertive – a creative commitment to make use of your situation, in a spirit of appreciation."

"I can't pretend to appreciate the flu, or flat tires, or other problems," I responded.

"This law is not about pretending anything, or denying your true feelings; it's about transforming them. You learn to surrender by shifting your perspective." The sage paced for a few moments, as if searching for the right words. "Look at it this way. If you were training in athletics, your coach might give you an award one day and demand a grueling workout the next. You could accept – even appreciate – all of this *as part of your training*. Well, the same is true in daily life. Spirit is your coach, Traveler, and life is your training. So I ask you, what if you *could* see a flat tire or the flu as an essential part of your learning and growth?"

"Well, I might as well view it that way. But I never pictured myself surrendering to a flat tire," I joked.

Smiling, the sage explained, "In its truest sense, this law guides you to surrender to the moment – to accept whatever arises, including your response to whatever arises. It means accepting not only life's ups and downs, but also accepting yourself – your body, your thoughts, and your feelings."

"Are you saying that once I learn to accept myself and surrender to whatever happens that life gets easier?"

"Life will continue to provide you with challenges and tests," she said. "But as you relax into life, even your difficulties will have a pleasurable aspect, like playing a challenging game or solving a puzzle."

"I can't shake the feeling that all this is much easier said than done."

"Everything is easier said than done!" she replied. "So begin in little ways. When you have a minor disagreement, acknowledge the other person's point of view and see what happens. Shrug off small disappointments. Follow the guidance of Epictetus, the Greek sage who advised his students, 'Learn to wish that everything should come to pass exactly as it does.'"

"Of all the laws I've learned, this seems the most challenging," I said. "It feels like I have to give up a part of myself—my desires, values, and preferences."

The sage's face shone with its own light as she answered. "The Law of Surrender honors the sanctity of each soul with its divine spark of individuality. You need not give that up, Traveler; you need only get out of your own way. Surrendering your smaller will to a higher will is not a common practice," she continued, "because you'd rather do what you prefer. This is understandable. But life doesn't always give us what we prefer, so our desires lead to attachment, anxiety, and frustration. Following your small will may lead to temporary satisfaction, but not to lasting happiness. When you see clearly that life is not only about getting what you want, but also about learning to want what you get, you'll align your life with the Law of Surrender."

"How do I actually practice this law?" I asked.

"Begin by asking, in any situation, 'What is for the highest good of *all* concerned?' This might mean praying for rain in your drought-stricken area even though your own roof is leaking. True surrender can be expressed in the heartfelt wish 'Not my will but thy will be done.'"

"That's going to be a stretch for me."

"A big stretch for anyone!" she said, smiling. "But stretching is a part of life. It begins by shifting your energy and attention from the desires of a smaller will to the wisdom of a higher will."

"Are you talking about the will of God?"

"Offering the prayer 'Thy will be done' does not require that you believe in an external God, only that you speak from your heart and ask yourself, 'If a wise, loving, compassionate God *were* guiding me now, what would I do in this situation?' Then feel your heart, and listen to your higher self; you will know what to do, and you'll find the courage and love to do it—because Spirit does indeed work through you, whether or not you are fully aware of it."

"I'm not sure how to begin," I confessed.

"Just open to life at whatever level you can. Over time,

the practice of surrender becomes deeper and more profound until you can embrace the rain clouds as you would
the pleasures of a sunny day. And remember to relax! Relaxation is the body's way of surrendering to the moment,
letting go of fixed ideas of what 'should' happen, so that
you can respond freshly and innocently to each moment,
without judgment or expectation."

Just then we looked up to see the cat who had taught
me about presence, sitting up tall on a nearby boulder.
"Her Majesty is holding court," I said.

The sage, of course, saw this as another object lesson.
"Have you noticed, Traveler, how cats will persist in going
where they want to?"

"Yes, I've noticed," I said, gazing up at the cat.

"But if someone is blocking their way," she added,
"they sit back, relax, let go, and take the opportunity to
lick their paws. Few people have learned the art of surrender as well as cats and masters of the martial arts."

"What does surrender have to do with martial arts?"

"The highest martial arts, like water, are flowing and
flexible, responsive rather than rigid or reactive. Such arts
teach us to pull when pushed and to push when pulled —
to blend with life's forces rather than wasting energy
struggling against them."

She stopped speaking and gazed up into the hills for
a few moments, then turned back to me. "Long ago in

feudal Japan, I was a young samurai, seeking mastery of the sword. I trained many hours a day, practicing cuts, parries, and evasive movements. I found a master who consented to instruct me, but he would say nothing about my technique, insisting that it was secondary. Instead, he emphasized the importance of relinquishing any attachment to victory, safety, or desired outcomes. Only the warrior who could let go of the smaller self with its desires, fears, and attachments would remain relaxed and focused. In a duel, surrendering to death meant survival; clinging to life meant losing it. Do you understand? This law has life-and-death practicality. The more you let go of attachments, the more you expand into greater freedom."

Anticipating my next question, the sage added, "Surrendering attachments doesn't mean giving away one's house or earthly goods; it's an internal act, a willingness to embrace whatever happens."

"*When*, exactly, does this law apply in everyday life?"

The sage laughed. "When does it *not* apply! Pick any circumstance you might normally reject, avoid, or resist; then surrender to it completely, turn it your way, and make the best of it. Surrender to your highest impulses as you work for positive change in your world. But, like the cat, don't waste energy resisting or fretting over circumstances you can't control."

We stopped to survey the rolling hills below. The sage

sat down on the grassy hillside, and I followed suit. Then, quietly, almost reverently she continued. "I acknowledge how difficult it is to surrender to life as it appears—to the greed, pain, and injustice in the world. In time, however, you will come to see everyone and everything as an aspect of Spirit—accepting on faith that despite our difficulties, everything in the universe is unfolding as it must. Surrender is an act of humility, an acknowledgment that life is a mystery whose depth the mind cannot fathom. As Isaac Bashevis Singer wrote, 'Life is God's novel; let God write it.'

"I can promise you this, Traveler," she concluded. "The Law of Surrender will show the way to a natural state of grace, opening the way for a flowering of faith, leading to the realization of your essential unity with all beings—an awareness so profound that it accelerates your evolution and catapults you on the path of human potential, into a spiritual reality existing long before the material world."

THE LAW OF UNITY

REMEMBERING
OUR CONNECTION

*We appear on Earth
as separate beings with diverse destinies;
but as each separate raindrop
is a part of the sea,
so are we each a part of
the Ocean of Awareness,
the Body of God.
Find love and inner peace
deep within the highest truth
that we are all one Family.
Leave behind the baggage
of fear, envy, and resentment;
fly aloft on wings of understanding,
to enter the boundless Land of Compassion.*

Ah, not to be cut off,
not through the slightest partition
shut out from the law of the stars.
The inner—what is it?
if not intensified sky,
hurled through with birds and deep
with the winds of homecoming.
—Rainer Maria Rilke

*C*louds blew in from the coast, bringing a quick shower and a rainbow to the northeast. As we paused at a scenic overlook, the sage spoke of the final law she was to share with me before our parting.

"The Law of Unity," she began, "presents a special challenge for both of us, because its transcendent nature makes it fully understandable only from a higher state of awareness. So, at first, I may touch only your mind. But my words are seeds; when they sprout forth and touch your heart, this law can transform your life forever. The Law of Unity calls forth the Great Realization that we are not as separate as we appear to be—that we are actually One Being, One Consciousness."

"No disrespect intended," I said, "but so what? I mean, what does this law have to do with everyday life?"

"This will become clear soon enough," she replied. "The Law of Unity isn't easy for the small self to grasp because it doesn't coincide with everyday perception. So let's first acknowledge that at the level of everyday reality, we do indeed have separate bodies, minds, and emotions. If I have a thought, it doesn't necessarily arise in your head at the same time; if I experience an emotion, you may not feel the same way; if I bruise my shin, you don't feel the pain.

"The Law of Unity is a paradox, you see—both false and true, depending upon our state of awareness. Whether we are One or many depends more upon our perspective than on any objective reality. Conventional knowledge tells us that we are separate; higher wisdom informs us that we are One. A shift of perception reveals that we are all the same Consciousness, manifesting in different bodies, the way leaves are part of the same tree. Humanity forgets to notice this higher truth, however, focusing instead on our differences, on our separation. But you won't forget, will you, Traveler?"

"I won't forget," I said. "But I'm not sure I fully understand it."

"At least we've taken a first step; let's see where the next one leads," she said, picking up an acorn from the forest floor. "If we examine this acorn, we call it 'one'; yet it's made up of millions of different cells, molecules, and atoms. We call a tiny atom 'one,' but it's also comprised of many particles and forces. If we examine the Earth, we call it 'one'; yet it's actually made of earth, air, fire, and water—including thousands of species, billions of living beings, and countless trillions of atoms. So, is an acorn, an atom, or the Earth one or many? And what of humanity?"

I had no answer; I could only ponder the question. "I guess it's a paradox," I finally said.

"Yes," agreed the sage. "And since that is so, you can *choose* how you will view reality—from a smaller or larger state of perception."

"Let's look at it another way," the sage continued. "Do you agree, Traveler, that language reflects our most fundamental perceptions—that the way we speak and the words we use have something to do with how we view our reality?"

"Yes, that sounds right."

"So when you say the words '*I'm going to my house*,' that sentence makes sense, doesn't it?"

"Sure."

"And the 'you' who refers to it as 'my' house is of course separate from the house. Correct?"

"I'm with you so far."

"Well, then, what do you mean when you say, '*My body feels good today*'? The 'you' who refers to it as 'my' body—is that 'you' also separate from the body?"

"Well, I never thought about it before. I guess it's just a convention of speech," I answered.

"Yes it is," she continued. "But you agreed that language reflects our fundamental view of reality. And this sentence clearly implies that 'you' are not your body, but something that 'has' a body."

"Yes, I guess it does."

"Is it possible that our language reflects a deeper truth? Let's take it a step further. If you are not your body, who are you?"

"Well, I guess you could say I'm a soul, or a higher self, that has a body or lives in a body—something like that."

"All right, then. But what does it mean if you refer to 'my soul' or 'my higher self'? *Who is this 'me'*?"

"I—I don't know."

"Could it be that the 'you' who speaks through the body, who refers to 'my' house, 'my' body, 'my' soul, 'my' higher self, is, in the truest sense, pure Awareness itself?"

"I—I don't know. It's a paradox—a . . ."

"Yes, it is, indeed. Consider it, Traveler! The Awareness that looks out through a billion eyes is the One Consciousness of infinite Love and Wisdom that we call God, who watches life unfold with mercy and compassion, and who is life itself. Could it be that even as you go about your daily business, with your personal desires and concerns and dreams, that you are that Awareness which also manifests as all these bodies and minds and trees and birds and acorns?"

"May I be excused?" I said. "My brain is full."

She laughed. "That's just the problem! Your brain cannot figure it out; you can only *feel* it or not. When you do, in rare and expanded moments, your mind will finally come to rest; you'll bathe in absolute bliss and experience pure peace and joy. Until then, these are only words."

I sighed, feeling as if I were missing something important. I wanted to experience what she was saying.

Again responding to my innermost thoughts, the sage lifted my chin and looked into my eyes. I gazed back, and found myself drawn in deeper and deeper, until her face began to change: First I saw light around her; then she was a very old woman, and then a fierce warrior, and then other people, too, until finally, I saw . . . myself. I don't mean my reflection; I mean that our connection was so deep that only one being was there, not two.

Then I snapped back to everyday awareness. We were sitting cross-legged in the soft grass. I was dazed and speechless. "That was only a preview, Traveler," said the sage. "I'm not asking you, in your everyday awareness, to experience or believe or fully understand your Oneness with all of Creation. That experience is only given by grace. But when you've felt that Oneness with even one human being, you can know it with the world. A part of you, a place deep within your heart, knows this higher truth; that is why you can, in any moment, align your-self with the Law of Unity by choosing to perceive other people—loved ones, friends, and adversaries alike—as aspects of your larger Self.

"So the next time you argue with someone," she continued, "or make love, or play a sport, ask yourself, 'What if I chose to see others as an aspect of me—chose to perceive us as One? How would I act? How might that influence my relationships? What then would happen to feelings of envy or jealousy? What would happen when my smaller self-interest became a larger Self-interest?' Would not competition become cooperation as you realized that even your adversaries were your students and teachers—a part of you?"

"It seems like it could change almost everything."

"This realization can indeed change the world, one soul at a time," said the sage.

"Some teachers and books refer to this idea of unity."

"Few have heard," she responded. "The world is only now growing ripe, nearly ready to understand—not just a few idealists, but a multitude of realists who recognize that human evolution—even human existence—depends upon this expanded vision of humanity as One. Just as our different organs cooperate for the good of the entire body, our world is on the cusp of a shift from competitive self-interest to openhearted cooperation in the interest of the Whole Body of Humanity."

In that moment I understood why she had first greeted me as a long-lost brother. The sage actually saw me, and everyone else, as a part of her. "You can understand," she said, speaking to my thoughts, "why life seems so humorous to me. Talking to you, looking at a tree, watching the deer, I see only another aspect of 'myself.' I pick berries, and it's like—"

"Like that J. D. Salinger story," I interrupted. "A boy drinks some milk and feels like he's 'pouring God into God.'"

"Yes, Traveler, it's just like that. And as you begin to see friends and adversaries, loved ones and strangers, through the eyes of the One Being, then all dilemma and conflict are dissolved, all wounds are healed, and all paradox is resolved in the light of this essential truth. This is the end of all seeking, because you *are* everyone and everywhere. It is the end of all fear, because you grasp as living truth who you are — that pure Awareness which never dies. In Unity is the completion of all the laws of Spirit: a state of balance and equanimity, perfect faith in the choices you make and the process of your life, patience as you walk step-by-step in the eternal present, compassion for all other aspects of your Self. Here, doubts are overcome, and all actions shine with integrity. After lifetimes of searching, you are at One with the universe."

The sage's voice grew softer, as if she were in a reverie: "Can you grasp it, Traveler? Can you feel the truth of my words? Do you understand that you are the burning child in a war-torn village, and you are the pilot dropping fire? That you are the mother and the newborn babe, the victim of a brutal assault and the rapist who commits the crime? All things done in the name of God or the devil you have done. The highest and most humble are you, wearing rags of torn cloth and robes of gold. You are in every act of kindness or cruelty, of cowardice or courage. Where goes the fool or the sage, and the creatures who walk or swim or fly, there go you. One and many, high and low, bitter and sweet, you are the Earth, and above, and below.

"You are the Light that shines through the eyes of all beings, truly One. That is how I know your thoughts and how I can speak of my 'past lives': Since we are One, we share *all* past lives, which are occurring now, since past, present, and future are also One."

"Do you mean," I asked, "that when I come to realize this unity as deeply as you, I'll also be able to tune into other people's thoughts and know past lives?"

"Of course!" she said, laughing. "You'll know anything you need know in order to serve others. But such powers will no longer concern you, because you will *be* everyone. Aligning your life with the Law of Unity changes everything even while everything appears the same. You live an ordinary life, as I do; you appear an ordinary person, yet the world becomes infinitely sweeter, more intense, beautiful, humorous, and peaceful."

We emerged from a protective ring of trees and started down the mountain, back to where I'd find the familiar path home, for we were nearing the end of our time together. As we walked, the sage wove a new vision of our future: "As a global consciousness awakens, Traveler, we find ourselves in the midst of a fundamental transition.

"This transition will not be without difficulties, but the Great Awakening is as inevitable as the last breath of the dying or a baby's first cry. As we speak, the illusion of separation is giving way to the higher truth of our unity. Now is the time to embrace the Earth, for soon, we will embrace the universe."

Epilogue:
The Sage's Farewell

Every now and then,
take a good look at something
not made with hands:
a mountain, a star,
the curve of a stream.
There will come to you
wisdom and patience,
and above all, the assurance
that you are not alone in the world.

—Sidney Lovett

As the sage finished speaking, we stepped onto a familiar trail, and I felt a sense of completion. "Does this mean my training is over?"

"You've completed the first important steps, but the journey never ends," she answered.

"What about the assistance you said you needed—the important mission?"

"That, Traveler, you and many other souls will come to understand in good time. The mission is happening even as we speak—all part of the Great Awakening. And now, I must go; there is a young woman in England I'm to meet soon, then a grandfather in Spain. A child in Germany awaits me, though she doesn't realize it, and there is an Iranian soldier now standing guard who calls silently to me. I feel the longing for which they have no words. And there are others, too, Traveler, waiting as you have waited."

"How can I ever thank you?" I asked.

"Live the laws," she said. "It is enough."

"I'll never forget you."

"When you remember the laws, you'll remember me." She placed her hands on my shoulders. Her eyes, filled with the light of compassion, looked deeply into my own. "Traveler, our time together has begun a graceful yet irreversible learning process. I have given you these laws not to bind you, but to free you. They come from deep within you; they are the alchemist's keys to love, freedom, joy, and fulfillment. They are the stepping-stones to your human destiny and what lies beyond.

"You don't have to remember these laws; you only have to live them, and they will transform your life. They are seeds, planted well and within you forever, waiting for the right time to sprout and grow, and they will—most assuredly they will—for the Gardener is always with you, providing whatever you need. These sprouts will blossom in their own good time, bearing fruits of courage, and love, and understanding.

"Nothing matches their power. And yet, they are all secondary to the Law of Love, for if you lose touch with your heart's wisdom, nothing else avails; if you love, nothing else is necessary. These laws will free the love trapped within you to expand into the world in joyous service for the common good.

"These are my wishes and prayers for you, all the days of your life: May you find grace as you surrender to life. May you find happiness, as you stop seeking it. May you come to trust these laws and inherit the wisdom of the Earth. May you reconnect with the heart of nature and feel the blessings of Spirit.

"The challenges of daily life will remain, and you will tend to forget what I have shown you. But a deeper part of you will remember, and when you do, life's problems will seem no more substantial than soap bubbles. The path will open before you where before there grew only weeds of confusion. Your future, and the future of all humanity, is a path into the Light, into a growing realization of the Unity with the Creator and all creation. And what lies beyond is beyond description.

"Even when the sky appears at its darkest, know that the sun shines ever upon you, that love surrounds you, and that the pure Light within you will guide your way home. So trust the process of your life unfolding, and know with certainty, through the peaks and valleys of your journey, that your soul rests safe and secure in the arms of Spirit. So be guided, as I have been guided, and know the peace of God."

Having spoken, the sage turned up the path and quickly disappeared. The sun was just breaking through the mist as I found my way down the hillside. I glanced back once, perhaps hoping to see the figure of a woman standing somewhere above, at the edge of the forest. But seeing only my own shadow, cast by the setting sun, I turned once again toward home.